The Giant, The Dream Machine and Me

Ginny Hartman

Acknowledgments

There are quite a few people without whom my fabulous six months in the USA wouldn't have turned out as they did. Firstly, I would like to thank Roger Hart for the two remarkable months I spent as his guest and employee in New York. If he hadn't done so, then I probably wouldn't have gone to Pennsylvania. I wouldn't have gone to Pennsylvania if my fellow student John Rue hadn't invited me up there and then I wouldn't have found a giant in the woods. Thanks John!

Big huge thanks to all of my friends who supported me through all the ups and downs of being a mature student. To Harvey and Judy Goodman who not only gave me a home when I had to give up mine but who also kept everything ticking over for me in the UK while I was off gallivanting. To Brian and Jane Kirk, John Foxon and the many other friends who helped me through those impoverished days and who supported me through my good times and dark times since. You know who you are.

Andrea Lucy-Hirst has been a trustworthy, honest and inspirational proofreader of this book, which she's probably sick to death of by now, I'm enormously grateful to her for all her support.

And last but by no means least my gratitude to George, my giant, with whom I had the time of my life and without him, I would just have caught a plane and wouldn't have had anything to write about.

1. Leaving Home

Summer 1990 and my life couldn't have been more different. This was my mid-life crisis, and I was loving every minute of it!

I'd morphed from a single parent with a 9-5 office job which I hated to a full-time student on a Creative Arts degree course at Nottingham Trent University. I'd made a dramatic and life changing decision. Who would have thought that a 41-year-old could transform from a legal executive in her neat M&S pleated skirt and matching jacket with patent kitten heels into a creative arts student in ripped jeans and Doc Martens, swapping one uniform for another!

My younger son had just flown the nest, his older brother had left a couple of years earlier and this was the first time in about 18 years that the only person I was truly responsible for was myself. My life couldn't be more different now. I'd completed my first year of uni and was very much looking forward to my second. I had been thrilled to bits to be offered the 'fall semester' on a student exchange programme at San Francisco State University in September. I couldn't wait! The student exchange office had actually asked me if I would like to go to San Francisco for four months! I didn't even have to think about it, I just said 'yes please'! They had only just started the exchange programme with SFSU, and they had asked me to be the first student to go there, on the premise that if anything went wrong, as a mature student I would be better able to handle it than a younger student. I thought, 'bring it on!' They even gave me money towards the flight, although I would have gone anyway!

Of course, with my only income being my student grant, I would need to earn some money through the summer. I was lucky that my secretarial skills had made me a popular 'temp' during the vacations. I'd heard English secretaries were in high demand in the USA and it occurred to me that I might be able to get a job there in the summer, rather than temping in an office in boring old Nottingham.

I'd never been to the States before, and I was determined to make the most of my few months there.

My childhood friend, Roger Hart, had lived in Queens in New York City for many years. I wrote to him to let him know my plans and that I was thinking about trying to get some work in the USA through the Summer before I started at San Francisco State that September and asked his advice on the best way I could go about it. Bless him, he was thrilled to hear from me, and he invited me to his home for the summer. Not only that, but he also said he would find me a job in his office at City University, New York, where he was a professor. So, now I would be time in New York as well as San Francisco! Funny how everything was falling into place to give me a wonderful, unexpected adventure.

Roger and I had grown up together, living on the same street and our Mums were best friends. He'd always said I was the first girl he ever kissed, when we were six and we had to hold hands when we crossed the road to school! In spite of that kiss having a lasting effect on Roger, it's a shame that I can't remember it but nevertheless, Roger and I had remained like brother and sister for all these years. He would make me very welcome when I arrived in New York as a USA virgin at the end of June 1990.

I'd let out my little Victorian terraced house for six months, which took care of the mortgage repayments whilst I was away. My only other income was my mature student grant of £3000 a year. A portion of that was paid termly, so I would get £1000 to cover all my living expenses for the four months I was at SFSU. Not a lot, even in the nineties!

I'd always been very hard up, bringing the kids up without any support from their father, who left when they were little, and I was used to getting called into the bank to 'discuss' my overdraft on a regular basis. When I got myself accepted at Nottingham Trent University, I had a different conversation with my bank manager. There was no online banking in those days, and you got to speak to a real person, usually the same person each time. I had built up quite a rapport with my bank manager, he was actually a very nice bloke, about my age. I had been called in yet again to get told off about my overdraft. Time to bite the bullet! I can remember now exactly what I said to him, I had practised it.

"Bill, I've been coming to see you like this for a very long time now, haven't I?"

He nodded and looked very serious.

"Because I've been in the poverty trap, with two kids and low pay, haven't I?"

He nodded again and there was a glimmer of sympathy on his face. He knew I wasn't stupid or careless, I just hadn't ever earned enough money to support myself and two kids by myself. This was a man who had seen me move from legal office to legal office just to get a salary hike of £500 per year. Who had discussed with me several times remortgaging my house to pay off my debts, which indeed I had done, just to keep my kids fed and my head above water.

"Well, I'm going to do something about it once and for all, would you like to know what I'm going to do?"

He smiled and said, "Indeed I would, Ginny."

I swear he thought I was about to announce I was getting married to a Man with a Good Job, as my mother was constantly telling me to do, instead I said, "I'm giving up work altogether!" and then I sat on my hands all scrunched up in my seat and held my breath for what seemed a very long time waiting for his reply, which eventually came: "Go on". I explained that I had got a place at university and was finally changing the direction of my life and all I would have for three years would be my mature student grant of £3000 a year. Then I waited again. Another long pause. Then he looked at me and to my amazement he said, "Well I think you're being very brave and I'm going to help you all I can"! I almost fell off my seat with relief and then threw myself on his mercy, asking about the best way to proceed and he confided in me that he too was having a midlife crisis and wished he had the courage to do what I was doing. I couldn't imagine him in ripped jeans and Doc Martens, frankly, but stranger things have happened! I mean, look at me!

And this conversation with this lovely bank manager, the species now sadly extinct, had helped me to get to where I was that summer in 1990. Prior to four months at San Francisco State University, I was spending a couple of months in Queens, NYC with Roger, helping with admin in his 6th floor office on the 42nd Street in Manhattan, with a spectacular close up view of the Chrysler Building out of my office window, always reminding me of where I actually was! Thank God for Bill Barclay!

I'd actually found suitable tenants for my house quicker than I expected and they were in a hurry to move in before I was ready to move out, really. I was rescued by my dear friends, Harvey and Judy Goodman, who had a granny flat and offered it to me for a few weeks until I was ready to fly, so that my tenants could take up residence. I'd warned the tenants that there might be a cat trying to get in the house. My next-door neighbour, Paul, had always looked after Miss Elsie when I went away. He loved her and I think she loved him too, so I'd asked Paul if he'd like to adopt my sweet little black cat. It wasn't fair on either of them to ask Paul to just look after her for six months, better for both of them to have some permanence in their relationship, I thought. It broke my heart to move her in with Paul, I'd had her for ten years, but he was delighted and promised me she would be fine. I knew that she would be happy with him but worried about her anyway. Would she understand what was happening?

So, the process began of getting my house ready for the tenants and packing all my stuff up that a) I didn't want the tenants to use, b) I needed to move to Harvey and Judy's, and c) was taking to the States with me. The lists were endless! At the same time as I was dealing with this upheaval, I had assignment deadlines looming that I had to crack on with for the end of my first year at Uni. Talk about high stress levels!

At the end of the summer term, after a few weeks of staying in Harvey and Judy's granny flat they gave me a brilliant send off, inviting all our friends to a brunch party, to see me off on my travels. My brother was there too; he was going to drive me to Heathrow later that day with my two huge suitcases. And my nineteen-year-old, Tom aka 'Mr Cool', was also there. His big brother had driven up from his home in Cambridge the day before to say cheerio as well. I wasn't worried about John, he worked for his Dad now, and lived with him so I guessed he wouldn't miss me as much as his brother would. Tom was still in Nottingham, living in a shared house in the city whilst he studied, and we would talk on the phone every day that we didn't see each other.

So, my departure from my hometown turned out to be an emotional affair with a big bunch of my favourite people standing in Harvey and Judy's front garden to wave me off. As I looked at this line of people waiting to give me a hug, I realised I was saying goodbye for six months to all of the people in my life who are dearest to me. It was a bit of a revelation as well, to see them emotional at my departure. I have to put the Atlantic Ocean between me and all my friends to realise how important we all are to each other! The general consensus amongst them, vocalised quite often during the course of the day, was how brave I was being. My view was that I was being brave before I had decided to embark on this change of life. By bringing up my two boys alone for most of their lives on not enough money, earned at a job that bored the arse off me anyway. For about 12 years overcoming the daily difficulties of juggling full-time work and parenting and just about keeping my head above water. That was brave! This was fun!

By the time I got to the very end of the hug line of my friends I was blubbing like a fool. At the end of the queue, right by my brother's car, was my lovely boy. I gathered him up in my arms and squeezed him and squeezed him. My friends were melting away from this scene, either with tact or embarrassment at watching me turn into a blubbering wreck. We had the biggest longest six-month hug and I swear my Mr Cool was trying not to cry. I couldn't let go of him. I was loudly sobbing uncontrollably with big gulps and snot and everything by then. Through my sobs, I said all the Mum things. 'Are you going to be ok?' 'I'll write as often as I can and phone when I get there.' 'Are you sure you're going to be ok?' 'Have you got enough money?' 'Don't forget to change your socks every day or your athlete's foot won't get better will it?' 'You will be ok, won't you?' 'Ring your dad if you've got any problems.' (I'd had sharp words with his dad, telling him to keep an eye on his youngest so whilst I was away, but he'd never shown much in the way of parenting skills before, and I doubted he would now.) Tom was putting a brave face on saying,

'Of course I will, have a good time Mum and write to me loads,' and this sort of conversation would have gone on for much longer, but my brother Nick had started tapping his watch and I tore myself away from my son. It wrenched my heart out, but I had a plane to catch. I was waving out of the car window till we were out of sight. We were halfway down the M1 before I managed to pull myself together and soon after that I was thanking my brother for the lift, negotiating Departures at Heathrow and hoping I wouldn't have to pay excess baggage charges.

2. New York

I'd never had jet lag before. 25th June 1990 was my first full day in New York, which started at 5.30am as I was already wide awake. I had a student visa and was required to spend my first night at the downtown YMCA and fill in various forms, promising I would behave myself, not overstay my allotted 6 months and attend an orientation meeting. I'd arrived at about 11pm, New York time but my body was telling me it was only 6pm and I was starving. The YMCA was a dump, and my room was a converted broom cupboard, I swear. I was glad that I would only have to stay there for one night. By 6.30am I was at a diner across the street, drinking coffee, eating eggs over easy, using my dollars for the first time and soaking up the New York atmosphere. Then back to the YMCA for the 9am orientation meeting, which was mostly stating the obvious, laying down the law about our length of stay and was quite boring to be honest. Most of it seemed irrelevant to me, yes, I would of course only be in the USA for six months and would be home by December. And yes, I would of course behave myself! It was a requirement fulfilled.

Next came my reunion with Roger, who I hadn't seen for years! He was asked to give his name and address before they let him take me away, in case he was a white slaver or something, I guess! It was lovely to see him again and we had a big hug before he said, 'let's get out of here'. I was very excited as he drove me through the skyscrapers of Manhattan. I was like a kid, pointing at everything and exclaiming 'oooo look' every five minutes, like he hadn't seen it all before, despite having lived there for about 20 years!

We arrived at his brownstone house in Queens. Stripped pine floors everywhere and big comfy Laura Ashley sofas and a big kitchen diner that led on to a small but beautiful garden. His parents owned a plant nursery when we were growing up. I should have known he'd have a garden, even in a city which was really short on gardens.

He made me a big pot of tea to make me feel at home and after a chat he said he had to go into work for a couple of hours. I was quite relieved actually, I was seriously flagging by then, so I used the time to unpack in the lovely room he'd given me, had a shower and then sat in his garden with another pot of tea and dozed until he came back. We talked some more and then he took me for a walk round the block and to meet his favourite butcher, Lou, and we bought a load of meat for the barbecue he was having that night to introduce me to his friends. As we talked it was apparent that he had a lot of women in his life and I was to meet three of them at the barbecue together with some other friends of his, all of whom were delightful and happy to make plans with me. All this about 36 hours after I was blubbing on my son's shoulder in Nottingham!

The next day, Rog took me into his office at City University New York to get me started as an admin assistant and to introduce me to his PA, Suzanne Rubinstein, who took me under her wing and became a great friend.

I had a blast with Roger who was happy to show me the city, accompany me to the theatre and we often went for dinner with friends. I asked him if he'd take me to Harlem because I wanted to take some photographs for a project for my art tutor back home. It wasn't very safe for this blonde, white woman to get out of the car in this area back then, so I stuck my head out of the sunroof and got some photos whilst Roger was driving slowly through the streets!

Roger was an eligible bachelor these days, this knobbly kneed boy who'd had to hold my hand when we walked to school together. It hadn't occurred to either of us to get together, we just didn't have that sort of relationship. But Toni, Lori and Shelley, some of his 'fan club' were keen to get brownie points from Roger so they befriended me and took me out and about when Roger was away, which was actually quite often. We did girly things like lunch in Central Park and Bloomingdales. A sunset cruise with Lori around the Statue of Liberty. Catching the ear-poppingly high speed lift with Toni up to the 103rd floor of the World Trade Centre to a cocktail bar where I had my first ever strawberry daquiri and watched the planes flying over New York below us.

We'd also watched yet another spectacular thunderstorm pass over the city from that magnificent building. Thunderstorms are very frequent in the summer and the average temperature is around 29C and the humidity is about 85%, most days, and there's not much let up at night-time either. My hair was a mass of frizz the entire time and my hands swelled up to the point that I had to have a ring cut off. The oppressive heat was exhausting and the air that clung to New York was thick and yellow. Although I was having a ball, I began to wonder if it would be good to get out of the city for a couple of days.

3. Pennsylvania

I'd dreamed of travelling overland from New York to San Francisco, to see as much of the States as I could but with very limited funds, I couldn't imagine it happening. I'd looked at Greyhound buses and trains but with the number of changes I would have had to make on that 3500-mile journey, I didn't fancy it on my own and had reluctantly concluded that it would be better to fly.

Then I found myself invited up to Milanville, Pennsylvania for the weekend to stay with a young chap called John, who I'd met when he was an American exchange student on my degree course in Nottingham and was now back home. He was in the year ahead of me at Nottingham Trent, and we weren't particularly friends. One lunchtime, in Nottingham, we were sharing a table in the Refectory, quite by chance. I was telling him of my plans to see as much of the States as I could whilst I was there and he gave me his phone number and said, 'come up to our place for the weekend'. He was about my son John's age, quite shy I thought, which he kept hidden by a brusque manner, but I liked him and we got to know each other a bit better. He made sure to seek me out on his last day in Nottingham to say he was hoping to hear from me when I arrive in New York. So, around 4th July, with Roger away again, I called the number that John had given me and plans were put in place for me to go and stay with him in his family home in a couple weeks' time.

I was so naive, I had to look at a map to see where Pennsylvania was in relation to New York. All I knew of the state was the city of Philadelphia so I could only imagine that I was going to spend the weekend in an apartment in the middle of another city full of smoke and sirens.

Roger's PA, Suzanne who I had been employed to assist, was married to Stan. He was a musician and was spending the summer working in the band at Browns Hotel, which was a huge and elaborate resort that mostly catered for Jewish families who would spend the summer there, in the Catskill Mountains in upstate New York (I learnt it was actually where Dirty Dancing was filmed!). Suzanne would spend her weekends driving up to visit Stan there. I had told her of my invitation to visit John in Milanville while we were having lunch with another new friend, Barbara, who was one of Roger's PhD students. Suzanne knew where Milanville was as it happened!   Before lunch was over a plan had been formed. Barbara was going to drive us up to meet Suzanne and Stan at Browns for lunch. Apparently, the resort/hotel was quite close to Milanville and only about a hundred and fifty miles north of New York. Another phone call to John and it was arranged that his parents would pick me up from Browns hotel in the evening. John had a job in a restaurant so I wouldn't be seeing much of him apparently. I was slightly anxious about spending the weekend with complete strangers; I didn't even know John that well, but I had resolved never to say no to any new experiences so here I was, a few days later, in Barbara's car driving north out of the city towards the Catskill Mountains, with the traffic getting less and less, the long quiet roads soon lined with fir trees and the air getting fresher and fresher. I could breathe again! It was about a two-hour drive before we arrived at Browns, which was a massive sprawling elaborate 450 room hotel and resort, just in time for lunch with Suzanne and Stan the piano man who accompanied the many big names who performed there at its nightly shows.

After lunch the four of us went to a filthy, grotty and quite wonderful bar, called 'Fishys' for the afternoon. Fishy was behind the bar, about 75 and very sprightly and also very cheeky and I loved him! Suzanne, Barbara and I talked all afternoon as we strolled through the lush grounds of the hotel and then went for a pizza. Suzanne had fixed us two singletons up with two singing brothers who joined us for dinner! Tom (mine!) was very sweet, a recent widower. Kevin (Barbara's!) was younger and full of chat. The six of us had a jolly pizza dinner together with lots of banter and laughter before all the fellas had to go off and get ready for their evening performances. I couldn't believe all the lovely people I was meeting!

As arranged, I'd called John's dad when I arrived to arrange a pick-up time, which would be early evening. He said on the phone 'I'll be in a red blazer' and I thought 'that's a colourful jacket, how jolly!' so I told him what I was wearing too, shorts and a t-shirt, and wondered why Barbara was laughing so much. I learnt that a 'Blazer' is the name of a car! Not, in fact, a jacket as I had presumed! So, when Bud and Ann Rue turned up to get me in a big red car, they were met by a bunch of people all laughing at me and pointing at his car, shouting 'Red Blazer'! And then they understood why I had described what I was wearing, which definitely started our first meeting with a smile.

I said my fond farewells to the folks I'd had had such a brilliant day with and left with complete strangers, Bud and Anne Rue, in their red Blazer to be driven to God knows where! Deep breaths!

When we arrived at their home, I was astonished to find I was staying in a beautiful 58 bedroomed period house, called 'Innisfree' on a hill surrounded by forests overlooking the Upper Delaware River. Innisfree was often overrun with guests retreating from the city and attending the summer camps, but not now. I was the only guest as far as I could see, except the place was so huge there may well have been other people staying in the enormous maze of a place and I wouldn't have

even known. The impressive grounds and woods which surrounded the house were the habitat of skunks, chipmunks, groundhogs and deer. Hundreds of bats lived in the barn and would blacken the sky when they came out at dusk. I felt as if I was taking part in a Walt Disney wildlife movie.

Milanville, Pa is a small, insular community in the Catskill Mountains, miles away from anywhere and about 50 years behind the times. If you walked down the hill from the house and crossed the bridge over the Upper Delaware River you were back in New York State. It was hard to get to grips with this wonderful, lush green landscape after six weeks in New York city, living in Queens and taking my life in my hands every day as I caught the 'F' subway to Grand Central Station to get to my job at CUNY on 42nd Street in downtown Manhattan, which was still not actually too far away.

Bud and Ann, turned out to be decent, warm and friendly backwoods folk and they made me more than welcome, expressing surprise that I was their age, they'd expected a student John's age to be visiting them for the weekend and there was a great deal of interest in how my life had got me to where I was now. We had a lovely evening talking until after dark. Then the silence at night after those weeks in New York, trying to sleep through the stifling heat and the sirens, and the lovely fresh smells of grass and trees and herbs and flowers. It was unbelievable!

The next morning, I met up with John again over an enormous family breakfast. He'd been working late into the previous night at the restaurant, although he was still happy to spend the morning driving me around the area, Narrowsberg for coffee and Homesdale for lunch. He was off to work in the afternoon, so dropped me off back at the house after lunch.

Bud and Ann were pleased to see my delight in the surrounding scenery, the river, the woods and hills, and the quaint little town nearby with its large wooden homes and buildings typical of the area, as well as their beautiful old house and grounds. Although I was majoring in Performance, part of the degree course I was taking for the first two years of my three-year course was visual art, within which I was studying photography. I was mostly a landscape photographer, so my Pentax was in overdrive here!

I'd spotted a little cottage in the forest that surrounded the house. That afternoon I was invited to help everybody to repair the fence around the vegetable patch in an effort to keep the pesky groundhogs away from their squash. It was there that I met the person who lived in that cottage. He was a big friendly giant, a watercolour artist who had very little money, apparently and who traded his paintings for things, and rent, and helped out around the grounds of this beautiful, unexpected place.

He was 6'9", I guessed he was a little bit older than me and he'd certainly lived a very different life to me, which made him fascinating. I loved his paintings and when he discovered I was studying the performing arts, he impressed me by telling me that he had been Tennessee Williams' set designer. He was very slow talking and ponderous, extremely gentle and gentlemanly too.

I liked him straight away. He had a whimsical way of talking to me and announced, quite randomly, that he was going to call me Sebastian! Turned out he was moving to San Francisco around the same time as me and was thinking about travelling overland. Over an excellent dinner with the family, I found myself, with much encouragement from John and his folks discussing with George the notion of us travelling together along the 3200 miles from New York to San Francisco by car, which we would buy between us. Quiet words with first Johns Mum and then his Dad assured me I would come to no harm with George. I didn't say yes straight away dear reader! Just as long as you know that I did sleep on the notion of buying a car and driving 3200 miles with a total stranger! Honest! What would Bill Barclay say!

Another day, another huge Milanville breakfast. Oatmeal, cereal, eggs, bacon, fried potatoes, muffins, fruit, coffee and juice to start the day in stark contrast to my usual start to the day back home, which was usually a cup of tea and a fag!

It was Sunday and there seemed to be some sort of service going on in one of the buildings that were dotted about in the grounds. Bud invited me to join them, so I did, it would have been rude not to. It was Unitarian Universalist apparently, which I had never heard of before, but I liked the notion that it was not attached to any religion, having had Methodism forced upon me as a child. There were about 10 people at the meeting and there was a lighting of candles and giving thanks for things, so I lit a candle and gave thanks for all the lovely friends I had made. Bud seemed pleased that I had made that gesture, which actually came from my heart.

After the service I was drawn to the little cottage in the woods to see what George was up to. I just wanted to see him, this man I had met 24 hours ago who called me Sebastian. The cottage was like a dolls house inside, with just a huge bed in the one room and a tiny kitchen. George was working on a watercolour landscape; There were beautiful paintings everywhere you looked. We talked again about driving to San Francisco together and I realised that I couldn't think of any reason why I shouldn't, but I could think of every reason why I should! He seemed sweet and gentle, and I trusted him. We agreed that I would leave him to look for a car that we could buy between us which we could sell upon arriving in San Francisco. We also agreed that we were very excited about the upcoming trip already!

I was back off to New York the next day. Roger was away but I had work to do in his office and wages to earn, I was now saving up for half a car! I had to tear myself away from this beautiful place. John had been itching to take a trip to New York so he offered to drive me back if I could give him a bed for the night, as I would be going back to an empty house it made sense.

As we left, I went to say cheerio to George, who said it was 'divine providence' that we had met when we did. I couldn't help but agree with him, this lovely giant who I'd found in a cottage in the woods. Something was telling me to grab this adventure with both hands. We swapped addresses and telephone numbers and I said bye for now to Bud and Ann Rue who'd made me so welcome at Innisfree, their home and off I went back to New York in John's pick-up truck. It didn't occur to me, until after John left after a could of days sightseeing around New

York with him, that I might be doing something very foolish. Just swanning acroos the States with a total stranger, and a giant to boot, what was I thinking? I was imagining the long-distance conversation, "Hi, its Mum, how are you? How's your athlete's foot? Are you still using that powder? Well, don't forget to change your socks every day! Just to let you know I've found a giant in the forest and am driving to San Francisco with him, it's only 3,200 miles." I could hear the shrieks of horror from here! I imagined the conversations back home, "Mother's taken leave of her senses, she should never have left that job at the solicitors office, let's get her home right now!"

Although, I also knew if I was to turn down the chance of this road trip from the east coast to the west coast of the USA with somebody who might actually keep me safe, rather than murder me en-route, then I would never have this opportunity again.

Roger was the first person I had to convince. He went all 'big brother' on me and made me promise that if anything went wrong on the road, "that's ANYTHING AT ALL, UNDERSTAND?" I would head for the nearest airport or train station and he even lent me a credit card, for emergency use. I was also made to promise to call him 'collect' as often as I could on my journey.

Sure enough, a couple of weeks after my first visit, I had a letter from George telling me he was looking at a 1977 Dodge Station Wagon for $600. A couple of weeks after that, grateful for the money I had earned in his office, I said a very fond farewell to Roger, with many promises to be careful and call him often and to not get into trouble. I left New York and headed off back to Milanville with all my worldly belongings.

I was good to go!

4. On Our Way!

Arriving back in Milanville was a joy. I'd caught the bus from New York and John had met me at the bus stop in Montecello in his pick-up truck, then we stopped on the way to Innisfree to buy a cool-box and drinks to put in the car for the start of the trip, which all of a sudden, was tomorrow! Then we drove past the house George was painting for a friend to earn money for the trip; a huge house covered in clapboard that he was painting white; it must have taken him weeks! It was nice to say hello to him, before leaving him to finish the job. I was greeted with open arms by Bud and Ann and quickly made to feel comfortable.

I was introduced to 'our' car, it looked a bit of a beast and would certainly be the biggest car I had ever driven. It had cost $600, and I had already sent him my half. George had built a large wooden crate over the roof rack to put all of his stuff in. When was I going to break it to him that I had never driven on that side of the car, or that side of the road before? At that stage I fervently hoped he was a patient passenger when it was my turn behind the wheel.

He finally got back to the house covered in speckles of white paint and after he'd got cleaned up, some guests started to arrive for dinner, friends of George's who had turned up to have a look at me and wish him bon voyage. I felt reassured that he had so many nice friends who clearly though the world of him.

We had an excellent jolly evening and George made us all laugh by stating he was very much looking forward to never going up a ladder to paint Barbara's house ever again! Apparently, he'd been at it for a month, just to earn money for the trip. I loved his dry sense of humour and his whimsy. He was calling me Sebastian again, I had no idea why, but I liked it! After dinner Ann helped me cut a large foam mattress into two pieces which would serve as our beds when we were camping on the road. George was busy loading his wooden crate on the roof rack with his artists' materials and other worldly belongings. We had decided over dinner to call our battered old Dodge the Dream Machine. How Californian!
I had a great night's sleep in that wonderful forest air, only disturbed by the sound of crickets and about 10,000 mosquitoes trying to get at me. Luckily, I was covered in insect repellent, having learnt my lesson when I was on my last visit. The next morning, after another massive Milanville breakfast and many fond farewells and wishes for a safe trip, we began our ten-day journey to San Francisco. It was Tuesday 14th August 1990. We had been given a load of fresh produce from the garden to help us on our way so after a few hours driving out of the Catskill Mountains through lush green forests and small towns, we made a stop to buy bread, cheese and mayo and found a picnic table where we stopped to have a picnic lunch.

I had already confessed to George that I'd never driven on the 'wrong side of the road' before, so he was expecting that he would need to be patient whilst I got used to driving the Dream Machine. The first thing we learnt was when one person is 6'9" and the other person is 5'4" and your car has a bench seat, that's going to be your first problem, right there! George had driven the first leg and the bench seat was pushed well back to accommodate his exceptionally long legs and I had enough space to throw a party in the passenger seat.

It was my turn to drive, with George's promise of a long straight road ahead as we hit Route 6 which is the longest two-lane highway in the USA, stretching all the way to California. It would be a much prettier way to go, he'd suggested, instead of miles and miles of boring freeways. With trepidation I got in the driver side of the car and found I couldn't even reach the steering wheel, let alone the pedals and when we moved the seat forward so that I could, my co-driver was all folded up with his knees under his chin in the passenger seat. Hmm!
After pondering this situation for a few minutes, we decided to get the two lengths of foam rubber that we would be sleeping on later out of the back of the

car and fashion them into booster seats for me. So, after pulling the seat forward a little bit, not too much, so that George wouldn't have to fold himself up in the passenger seat, we folded, pummelled and poked at the mattresses until they stayed where they were put, and I could sit on them to reach the pedals. The mattresses were memory foam and they clearly had no memory of being folded up before, so it was a bit of a battle! I suppose that was the first part of our learning curve with the Dream Machine over, there were to be quite a few more.

So, with me driving the Dream Machine quite slowly for the first time, and George biting his lip in the passenger seat, we hit Route 6 and were heading for Ohio! That's when our elephants appeared, George said they were circling around us as I started the car and they were now over there, under a tree. I looked to where he was pointing and agreed they were fine looking elephants. Of course, there was nothing there, but the fantasy elephants appeared every day of the trip and we enjoyed their company.

We had a fair bit more of Pennsylvania to get through first and we also made a slight detour to visit East Smethport, a sentimental journey for George who used to live there. We stopped for dinner at what had been his favourite restaurant and he got quite emotional to be back there once again. No doubt I would find out what his attachments were when we were back in the car; we were certainly doing a lot of talking whilst driving!

Then it was time to find a campsite for the night. I was a bit nervous about how this was going to work - me spending the night in a makeshift tent with George where close proximity was going to be unavoidable. We found a secluded campsite with a primitive toilet and shower block in it, deep in the country. George produced a large tarpaulin from the cavernous boot (oh sorry, the trunk!) of the Dream Machine and proceeded to tie one end of it to the roof rack and the other end to pegs hammered into the ground. He then laid a groundsheet down while I got my 'booster seats' out of the car and there they were, mattresses again!

After subjecting myself to the grim toilet and shower block with no hot water and covering myself in insect repellent, wondering if I would have to repel anything else overnight, I crawled under the tarp and into my sleeping bag, which I zipped right up in spite of the warm night and humidity and said goodnight to George, on his foam mattress about six inches away from me, turned with my back to him and pretended to be asleep.

I must have eventually dosed off, in spite of his snoring, because I was woken in the small hours by George shaking me and whispering, 'I think there's a bear outside!'. We both lay there with our eyes wide open and our respective sleeping bags pulled well up to our chins, as if that would stop a bear from killing us in our beds, listening to munching and trampling noises outside of our very flimsy shelter until it got light. Seems George was no bear hunter, just a teddy bear, and I was just a wimp when it came to sleeping in the open anyway! I had never been camping before, I'm the sort of gal who prefers a clean bed with some sort of en-suite arrangement. I'd never been intrepid before and this night was certainly throwing me in at the deep end!

As dawn broke, we plucked up the courage to stick our heads out and saw our 'bear' which was in fact a horse, grazing quite close to the Dream Machine in the next field! George remarked that it seemed to be completely ignoring the elephants that he was sharing his field with!

So, that was our first night over thank God. George had been a perfect gentleman, but always the wimp, I wasn't sure I could sleep under the tarp every night for the rest of our journey. We got our makeshift camping equipment into the back of the car, making sure the mattresses were at the top of the pile for ease of access when it was my turn to drive.

Back into East Smethport for a diner breakfast (and clean toilets where I got a bit of a wash) and to look for the house where George's grandfather had lived - he was happy to have found it.

Then we were off again, driving through miles and miles of mountains, lakes and pine forests, heading for Ohio. Just one more stop in Pennsylvania. We had hit a town called 'Warren' which was my maiden-name, so we stopped for coffee and for me to buy a postcard that said 'Warren Pa' on the front to send to my mother: 'Guess where I am Mum!' I stopped short of writing 'wish you were here'. Heaven forbid!

5. Ohio

It was my turn to drive again, so the mattresses were duly pulled out of the back and pummelled into submission on the driver seat. The elephants were down near the river that morning.

We learnt that George gets very nervous when I'm driving through a town, as do I if I'm honest, not being familiar with the road signs doesn't help. The only time George had raised his voice on our journey was when I failed to stop at a Stop sign, not a traffic light, just a stop sign. I hadn't stopped because there was no traffic at all on the road in any direction, but apparently, I should have stopped anyway! Another lesson learnt! After that we agreed that I would only drive the long straight roads from now on, which was fine by me and anyway the long straight roads comprised most of our journey.

We had driven 381 miles that day and realised we were still learning things about the Dream Machine. Today we learnt that it is an oil guzzler, we had to buy a gallon of oil, half of which went straight into the engine. We also learnt that the suspension wasn't too great. With all of George's worldly goods in his crate on the roof rack, and all my stateside worldly goods in two large suitcases in the back, plus all our travelling and camping gear, we were seriously overloaded and if we went above 60mph the Dream Machine would rock from side to side rather alarmingly. We did wonder if we had an elephant on the roof and the next time that we stopped we did actually check - there was no sign of one! Good job we weren't in a hurry!

We arrived in a little town called Wauseon, Ohio just in time to find a place to pitch our tent for the night, just before it got dark. We managed to find a campsite marginally better than last night (the toilets had been cleaned that day at least!) and pitched our tent quite quickly. We had stopped to eat at a diner earlier and decided we would open the bottle of wine that Bud and Ann had given to us for the journey. We agreed it was the most terrible wine we had ever tasted, but we finished off the bottle anyway. It loosened our tongues a little bit and we stayed up talking until quite late. George heard about my disastrous love life, as most people did after I'd had half a bottle of wine. Then he shared with me that he was gay and with that out in the open we were much more relaxed with each other. We made each other laugh so much and I thought at that time that we would always be close friends. I loved his lovely deep voice and gentle protective manner – I was almost sorry he wasn't straight but anyway, there wouldn't have been any point in starting anything with him as I was going home at Christmas.

After a relatively comfortable night without too many threats from wild beasts, except of course the ubiquitous pesky mosquitos, we left Route 6 and took Route 80 to Chicago to save a bit of time. We lost an hour on the journey; we were in a different time zone now! I was getting more confident about driving and did about 200 miles along the freeway. When we hit Indiana, I noticed how the terrain changed as soon as we left Ohio. The minute we drove past the 'Welcome to Indiana' sign the landscape changed from miles and miles of flat cornfields to gently rolling hills and trees. We chatted about how the elephants were thrilled with this new terrain!

6. Illinois

We hit Chicago around lunchtime, Lake Superior looked like an ocean! After a Chinese lunch we split up for the afternoon because I wanted to look around some galleries that had been recommended to me by my art tutor back home. I looked around the Art Institute and then walked ten blocks to the Contemporary Museum of Art, which didn't impress me all that much but the walk there was great, and I got a real feel for Chicago which is pretty magnificent.

George and I met up again after I'd had my culture fix. I was touched at how George's face had lit up when he saw me walking towards him after our afternoon apart. We headed out of the city, and I took in the scenery along the way. Chicago is extremely photogenic with a lot of old buildings and skyscrapers, even more so with those huge thunderclouds forming overhead.

He drove us out of the city and onwards, until about 10pm when we found a camping ground, Rolling Oaks, which had a huge pavilion to camp under, which was fortunate because the rain was torrential by this point and it's safe to say our makeshift tent certainly wasn't waterproof! The noise of the lashing rain on the pavilion roof and splashing on the ground very close to us made it difficult to sleep under our tarpaulin and I started to long for a motel. Mercifully, we managed to keep dry. I worried about the elephants, but we decided they'd found shelter nearby. Our sleeping bags were very close together for warmth and we ended up as two well wrapped spoons. I could sense George breathing into my hair as he slept so I snuggled in a bit closer. It was lovely.

We had done 296 miles that day and another quart of oil had gone into the Dream Machine.

It was still raining when we left Rolling Oaks, Illinois in the morning, so we drove straight to the nearest diner for breakfast. At this stage in our journey through the Midwest, we were used to creating a bit of a stir when we walked into local diners, I suppose we did look like a bit of an odd couple, an aging hippy who would block out the light wherever he went and a prissy little Englishwoman who stood in his shadow. At this diner, I went to the counter and said, 'could I have two cups of coffee please' in my best British and the woman behind the counter couldn't understand me! "What she say?" She said to George, who chips in with "she asked for two coffees" and I said, "that's what I said!" and the whole thing turned into a comedy routine with much hilarity all around the diners. Of course, I played up to it a bit and the result was a very jolly breakfast with explanations about where we were headed and what I was doing in the States and many waves and 'safe travels' wishes as we left the diner, after a rubbish night it was a good start to the day. I was having a brilliant time again!

After miles and miles of driving through cornfields in the pouring rain, the wipers could hardly cope with the deluge, the sun suddenly came out. It was time to change drivers, so we pulled off the road and were surprised to find ourselves in what had once been and old drive-in movie theatre. There didn't seem to be anyone about but parked in front of the cinema screen was a Jaguar car, one of the first ever built by the looks of it, the likes of which I had never seen before in a place the likes of which I had never been before either.

As I got busy with my camera a young guy came out from behind the screen and said, "if you like that, come and look at this". George and I followed him to the back of the movie screen and into his workshop, well hidden from the road by the enormous concrete cinema screen. We were amazed to see his car, a 1922 Model T Ford in its original condition and looking immaculate. I'd only ever seen one in a silent movie before. It transpired the car was in perfect working order and the owner of it, Laurie, was as interested in us as we were in him and his eclectic mix of vehicles, ranging from vintage cars to racing tractors, in particular the one in front of us. He invited us to take a tour of Galesburg in his pride and joy and have lunch with him while his brother, Ronnie would fix some new shock absorbers to the Dream Machine. We, of course, were thrilled to accept and duly drove off to Galesburg which wasn't far, squeezed into the back of his marvellous car, like Laurel and Hardy, with George all folded up again. As we hit the town and approached the first traffic lights our new friend Laurie told us a Model T Ford didn't have brakes and the only way to stop it was to throw it into reverse. We just held on tight to the seat in front and hoped for the best, with Laurie laughing out loud at us!

We had a good lunch in Laurie's favourite diner and then he drove us back to his movie theatre garage/antique car lot where we gave his brother Ronnie $37 for fitting the new shock absorbers on the Dream Machine and said our grateful farewells to these lovely midwestern hillbillies.

It was my turn to drive and Ronnie and Laurie were laughing out loud as they watched us creating my booster seat! Great fun and new friends made, as well as another crazy experience for my diary!

By now, the weather had turned very hot and sunny and I drove us all the way through Illinois. I was excited to drive across the Mississippi River and we stopped on the bridge so that I could look at it and I was thrilled to see a real steamboat with the big paddle wheels rotating on it, passing sedately under the bridge we were standing on. Then onwards again, into Iowa and we kept on driving, apart from a break by a lake to cool off. We stopped in Uttomwa for dinner and then went on into the night.

336 miles today, and a deepening friendship. And elephants; we wondered what they were up to today. George was still calling me Sebastian, so I announced I would call him Sebastian too and for differentiation he would be Sebastian Blue and I would be Sebastian Cerise. I was just loving the pure daftness of it all!

7. Iowa

I was astounded by the starry sky, many millions of stars to see with no light pollution here on this very clear night, as if you could reach up and touch them.

We arrived at Red Haw National Park at around 1am, having tried and failed to find a motel, much to my disappointment. It would have been lovely to have a clean bed to sleep in and at least one shower after four sweaty days on the road. I could even rinse a few things through if I just had my own sink overnight! Ah well.

We were both extremely tired after a very long day following a sleepless night, so pitching our tent was a bit stressful, but we still managed a few laughs before we hit our respective mattresses and slept very well, in spite of the thousands of mosquitoes that seemed to have followed us from Pennsylvania. We were spooning in our sleeping bags again and I woke in the night to find my giants arm round me. I slipped my hand into his and that's how we slept that night. It felt very warm and comforting. I reminded myself that George had said he was gay.

Nebraska tomorrow and the first stop would need to be a garage for more oil.

Waking up in Red Haw State Park, Iowa was amazing us with its incredible beauty, we hadn't seen much of it the night before whilst we were looking for a place to stay in the dark. This morning, it was hot and sunny and we drove quite slowly out of the park taking in the sights, the deer wandering along the side of the road, the buzzards flying high above us and then miles upon miles of never-ending cornfields. I could see George was getting a bit fed up with having to stop the car to let me take yet another shot of this fabulous landscape. So, we pressed on to breakfast in Osceola with its brightly coloured old buildings beckoning to my Pentax. How I wish digital photography had been invented back then, it would have saved this impoverished student a fortune in Kodak film, developing and printing!

It was my turn to drive again after breakfast and we hit the road out of Iowa towards Nebraska for a couple of hours, then over the Missouri River stopping on the other side for lunch, which we agreed was truly terrible and was definitely not a good first taste of Nebraska!

George took over the driving again, and we hit Lincoln, Nebraska at about 4pm and joy of joys, we found a motel room! I was thrilled to be in a proper room with air conditioning, its own bathroom, two queen sized beds, a coffee machine, no mosquitos and the added bonus of a laundrette over the road! Funny what you learn to appreciate after five days of sleeping under a tarpaulin attached to a Dodge Plymouth!

213 miles today.

8. Nebraska

This room also had the luxury of a phone, so I made a couple of calls home, which made me suddenly homesick, plus a collect call to Roger who was reassured to hear from me that all was well, and that George and I were becoming great friends.

I got straight in the shower and luxuriated in washing my hair, letting the hot soapy water wash over me for a long time. George went for a walk to check out the town and probably the restaurants, knowing him as I did by now, he certainly loved his food.

I'd brought all my luggage out of the Dream Machine into the hotel room, in spite of us only staying one night. We had learnt that one of the back doors of the Dream Machine didn't lock so I was reluctant to leave any of my belongings in there overnight. It hadn't really mattered before now because until now we had never left the car in a car park and slept elsewhere. George's stuff was ok, in the padlocked crate on the roof rack and it wasn't as if the car looked like it was worth pinching, just easy to break into. Having my suitcases open in the room gave me the opportunity to change all my clothes and get across to the laundrette to wash everything I had been wearing on the journey so far. I was still a provincial gal who likes to be 'clean on' at heart! I enjoyed being in the laundrette which seemed to be Lincoln's social hub. I chatted with the locals, while they were having a beer and watching the huge TV on the wall as they waited for their laundry. It was lovely to have the smell of clean clothes again!

When I got back to the motel room George was back from his walk around the town and having coffee and pie, apparently. He had noticed there was a Summer Stock company production happening that night. It was 'True West' a play by Sam Shephard, so we decided to go.

I decided to have a bubble bath, just because I could and I wore some smarter clothes than George had ever seen me wearing before. When I was ready to go, with my look completed with makeup I noticed a different look in his eye when he saw me sparkling clean, freshly shampooed, glowing from the long bubble bath and all dressed up. 'My, don't you look gorgeous' were the words that came with that look, which surprised me a little bit. I just laughed it off at the time and teased him about wearing his one and only tie and off we went on our first Saturday night date at the theatre. He'd mentioned that he had seen the elephants queuing up to go through the car wash when he was out on his walk; we agreed that they had got a bit scruffy.

George said he was a bit short of cash, so I bought the tickets on the door. The play was truly terrible! Lousy acting and a rickety set, but we kindly agreed the script was 'interesting'. We went for a plate of spaghetti and a glass of wine afterwards and pulled the performance to pieces. I was enjoying the way he was looking at me across the candlelit table. And was he flirting?

Then, he made his announcement. He was now completely out of money. All the money he had made from painting Barbara's house was now gone and it transpired that was all the money he had. He had very high hopes of selling paintings and getting work when we reached San Francisco, but until then he had nothing but the loose change in his pocket. Zilch. We had casually taken it in turns to pay for things without much discussion needed and it had worked out fine up until now. We were literally half-way across the States to our destination so there was no point in turning back. I don't think George ever understood that I too was very hard up, existing as I was on my mature student grant with ongoing expenses back home. Clearly, I hadn't understood that he was flat broke either. We'd had more important things to talk about so far, like sunrises, sunsets, scenery, elephants and where we were going to eat and sleep next. The only thing I had, which he didn't, was an overdraft facility and one credit card, thanks to good old Bill Barclay, but it was already getting a severe hammering.

Halfway across America on my way to study the Arts at San Francisco State University, with a man I was getting very close to, gay or not, and a battered old banger as our only means of completing our journey. I was a very, very long way from my previous life working at Cleggs Solicitors in the middle of Nottingham! Thank God!

I wanted to keep going with my Sebastian Blue, we couldn't give up now, and what would I do if I did? Head for the nearest airport and fly over Colorado, Nevada and The Rockies instead of driving through them? It was a no.

I doubted if I would save much money if I did make my own way to San Francisco anyway and what would George do, stranded in Nebraska with the Dream Machine without money any to fuel the gas tank and his huge appetite? The thought of leaving him was utterly unacceptable anyway. It was a no brainer.

George was watching me anxiously as I pondered all this whilst I picked at my salad. I looked up at him and explained that I was broke too but I wanted to complete this journey of a lifetime with him and that I would find a way to pay for everything for now. He happily insisted that I make note of all the expenses and he would pay me back his half as soon as he was able to. I just secretly hoped my credit card would stand the strain and my cheques wouldn't bounce. Under the new regime, we ordered another glass of wine to celebrate. He raised his glass to me and said he couldn't have wished for a nicer travelling companion. I said' 'mutual, I'm sure' in my best New York accent and we laughed, and the mood was lightened once again.

I paid the restaurant bill and we wandered back to the motel. We luxuriated for a while before bed and then I realised I wouldn't need to be sleeping in my clothes tonight (as I had done when we were under the tarpaulin), so we had a bit of awkwardness while I went into the bathroom to change into a t-shirt for sleeping in. The atmosphere between us was changing and I was a bit confused. I decided I must be imagining things, George was gay! Wasn't he? We each got into our queen-sized beds and looked at each other over across the gap between us without speaking for quite a long time.

The moment passed eventually, then I said, 'Goodnight Sebastian Blue' and he said, 'Goodnight Sebastian Cerise' and we both had an excellent night's sleep in our individual, huge beds. No mosquitos, no sounds from crickets outside, I even slept through George's snoring!

It was lovely to wake up in the morning and use the coffee machine. It was all very relaxed in the room and suddenly we found ourselves having a very clumsy and frustrating cuddle! Just a cuddle, but it didn't feel platonic; his giant arms wrapping around me felt very good indeed. However, when we unlocked ourselves we needed to get on, check out of the motel before 10am and get going. George left me to go out and get himself some breakfast (it was a bit awkward giving him $10 out of my purse but it soon became the norm) while I had another shower and packed up my suitcases before we hit the road again.

We had done 1482 miles so far, so we had roughly another 1000 to do before we hit California. Next stop Colorado!   George was driving as we hit the freeway because we agreed Nebraska was nothing more than a place for us to get through.

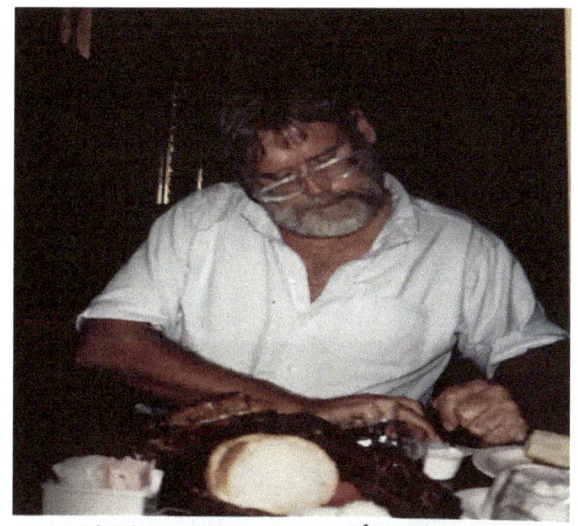

I am going to have a better nutritional diet for the remainder of the trip.
— *S. Melvin Baelen*

Dinner: $14

George: $10

Lunch: $8.40

Motel: $37

Gas: $15

That was the first financial entry in my diary, which George had insisted on.

9. Colorado

After a brilliant night's sleep and a shower, shampoo and a bath, not to mention my trip to a laundrette, I felt much more relaxed, comfortable and fragrant than I had since our trip had begun as we hit the freeway out of Nebraska. George was relaxed and happy as well and we got very silly in the car, with lots of vulgarity and screaming with laughter about very little. We'd both noticed how the sun was bouncing off the elephants now that they'd been through the car wash.

We agreed Nebraska was to be the State of terrible food, except for today's lunch which was a massive BLT from somewhere along the freeway which George pronounced 'real good'. I had started to notice how he was quite preoccupied with food (especially now I was paying for it all!) But he was a giant after all and giants take a lot of filling up, I suppose.

When we hit Colorado after a boring drive on the freeway to get out of Nebraska, which was flat, colourless and relatively uninteresting, the terrain suddenly changed into a prairie, stretching out for miles into the distance whichever way you looked with one highway cutting through it. The only relief from the miles of scrubland, desert and the long grey ribbon of highway stretching further than the distant horizon, was thousands of brilliant yellow sunflowers growing wild and lining both sides of the road.

After we had been driving for a few hours, (and we gained another hour by driving into a new time zone) without any noticeable change of scenery, we came upon a 'rest area' which was an unmanned lay by consisting of loos, a payphone and some picnic tables. Nothing else but useful, nonetheless for long distance travellers like us. We gratefully pulled in, to stretch our legs and use whatever facilities were available to us.

It was approaching 6pm on a hot and sunny Sunday evening. We wandered around for a while, glad to use our legs for a change until we noticed the Dream Machine had emptied its radiator all over the ground! The middle of nowhere was not a good place for this to happen! George had taken the precaution of joining the American Automobile Association before he left Pennsylvania so he got on the payphone to them, but I could tell by the look on his face when he came back from the phone that it was not good news. He had learnt that the Colorado AAA did not recognise the Pennsylvania membership and would not come out to us with a new radiator hose!

There was only one thing for it, George would hitchhike to the nearest town, which we guessed was about 20 miles away, to try and find a garage open on a Sunday evening that would sell us a radiator hose, then hitch back again. We had agreed that I would stay with the car with all our worldly possessions in it with that back door which we couldn't lock.

I put my best British stiff upper lip smile on and said, 'of course, I'll be ok!' with a magnificent display of phoney confidence as I gave him all the cash that I had to buy a radiator hose: 'Off you go, I'll be fine!' Nothing to it really, being left in the middle of the prairie whilst your travelling companion disappears into the distance with his thumb sticking out, your only protection being a car which doesn't lock all the way round. Piece of cake.

I decided to keep busy. After all, it had been a while since I had taken any photos and the sun was setting and the sky over the prairie was a vast expanse of gorgeousness, not only with the vibrant and ever-changing colours of the sunset, an added bonus, I could also see an electric storm happening miles way, lighting up that bit of sky. There was plenty more. I forgot that I was all alone in the middle of nowhere when I was taking in this magnificent view and photographing it until I ran out of film.

Then it was dark, and reality hit me. When I say dark, I mean pitch black, no lit roads across the prairie! Just the trillions of stars and the occasional flash of lightning to illuminate the vast expanse of prairie I was stuck in for an indeterminate length of time. I got back in the car for safety and after a little while a huge truck pulled in and the driver got out. I had sunk down in the bench seat hoping he wouldn't notice that there was a woman sitting in this elderly car that had wet itself. He gave the Dream Machine a cursory glance as he came out of the loo and climbed back into his cab, all he wanted to do was to get back on the road and on to the next town, as did I. Nothing to see here. I gave a sigh of relief as I watched his taillights disappear into the distances and carried on anxiously sitting there in the dark feeling a little anxious. I was hanging on to the door which didn't lock (like that would really help if some large woman eating prairie beast or mad axeman really wanted to get at me) for what seemed like hours until I spotted headlights coming towards me and held my breath until a car pulled in. I peered through the darkness until, with great relief, I could make out the unmistakeable silhouette of a giant in the car headlights, walking towards me. It was my giant, carrying with him a new radiator hose. I sprang out of the car as he got nearer and then he rushed towards me with his big bear arms outstretched and gathered me up in them. I fell into the hug and we held on to each other for the longest time, standing in what was left of a radiator puddle, without speaking. It was then, I think, that we both knew something else was happening.

It didn't take George long to fix the car and then we were happily on the road again. He told me about how anxious he was about leaving me and how he'd never been so relieved to see me when he got back to me and the Dream Machine, I said I had felt the same and we agreed that we deserved another motel that night.

We soon hit Sterling, Colorado and checked in to a motel imaginatively called 1-76 Inn. George was, as usual, thinking about eating, so we headed into town to find somewhere to eat. After a truly terrible dinner, we had a look round Sterling and found a fairground to wander round, just a leg stretching exercise really after sitting down all day, driving the Dream Machine. Then we realised that neither of us could remember where our motel was! We drove around Sterling for ages in a spectacular thunderstorm until we finally found our room for the night. For some reason we had found our predicament hilarious and were screaming with laughter at each wrong turn we took!

When we were finally in our motel room we agreed that we had hated being separated when the Dream Machine broke down and George was adamant that he would never leave my side again. We only used one of the beds that night. We just wanted to be close to each other. There wasn't a lot of physicality, but we knew it would only be a matter of time.

Gas $6

George$10

Lunch $15

Gas $15

1-76 Inn $38

Radiator Hose: $35

10. The Rockies

The next morning dawned and the storm had cleared and left Sterling sparkling in the sunshine. We did a fair bit of gazing into each other's eyes when we woke up, like star crossed teenagers, instead of a couple of forty somethings who really should have known better. Then we hit the miles of straight road across the prairie once again until we hit the Rocky Mountains. We stopped for a picnic lunch by the side of a stream with a pine forest and mountains all around us, so different from just a few miles ago, and quite magical.

Then we just started out on a long, slow drive up through the Rockies. We were getting higher and higher and my ears were popping. We didn't speak too much because we were so overwhelmed by the scenery that I almost cried, I was so emotional at the breath-taking beauty surrounding us. I was so grateful to be in its midst, and so thankful for the romance of this journey with George, in every sense.

We made stops where we could so I could take photos and I used up three Kodak 36 films! How I wish now that digital cameras had been invented, but this was 1990, no digital cameras, no emails and no mobile phones. We were in the dark ages, photographically speaking!

The weather had changed dramatically through the afternoon. We were 12000 feet above sea level by this point and it had turned quite cold and was pouring with rain. We stopped quite early for the night in a tourist trap called Grand Lake Colorado. We checked into a motel again The Inn at Grand Lake, where the blurb on their leaflet says:

"Trout leap only a few feet away from your canoe in the lake's early morning calm. A herd of elk breaks through the pine forest and into the sunlit meadow before you. A bald eagle cries overhead. Bighorn sheep peer at you curiously from craggy masses of ice and rock. The air is clean and crisp, the waters are clear and cool. The world about you is quiet, and yet pulsating with life. This is Grand Lake and surrounding area, the Jewel of the Rockies."

Just about sums it up. Except it was pouring with rain so we were grateful that The Inn at Grand Lake had a room for us to check into. We went for dinner and a wander around the village and then we turned in early because we were both very tired.

I also bought a few postcards to send home.

Home. My kids, my degree course, my mum and my house. All a very long way away. Bit of a reality check there. I was trying not to get too carried away with the notion of staying here for ever with George.

201 miles today.

> Hotel: $38
> Gas: $11.25
> Oil: £15
> Lunch: $5.75
> Groceries: $31
> Rocky Mountain Pass: $5
> Gas: £11.50

11. Utah

It was still cold and cloudy the next morning, we were about 12,000 miles up in the Rocky Mountains of Colorado, and after breakfast we started the descent towards Utah, using the brake much more than the accelerator. I let George drive that bit as the mountain roads were a bit hairy, we did it in a reflective and companionable silence. George needed to concentrate on the long narrow and winding descent, often with hairpin bends and long stretches where the road just dropped away on one side. As the Dream Machine rocked and rolled its way down the steepest mountain roads, I noticed some gravelled ramps which led off the road at regular intervals. George explained that they were called runaway truck ramps. Sometimes a truck's brakes would burn out as it negotiated this very steep and winding road and rather than let it run on down, out of control, mowing down any cars in its path, it would pull off the road to a stop in this ramp. Hairy! I fervently hoped the elderly Dream Machine's brakes would stand the strain of this part of the journey.

I was happy to be a passenger as it gave me more of an opportunity to take in the view of the lakes and mountains and notice how the weather was changing as we descended until we regretfully left Colorado and hit Utah where it was hot and sunny again and we had to make a stop to peel off a couple of layers of our warm clothing. As we got lower and the terrain was a more relaxed drive, we started talking once again. We had already had conversations about where I had planned to stay when we reached San Francisco when I would become an undergraduate at San Francisco State University for the Fall Semester. I'd opted not to stay in one of the halls on the campus. I couldn't face the thought of sharing a dorm with a bunch of girls half my age. My dear old friend Roger back in New York had a friend called Dave, who lived in Mill Valley on the outskirts of San Francisco and who had a granny flat attached to his suburban house that he shared with his wife. They had agreed to let me rent it until Christmas, when I would be flying home. Well, that had been the plan to start with anyway.

George was house-sitting for a couple of artists who were going to their holiday home in Greece for the winter and had asked their old friend to look after their house, rent free, until they got back in the Spring. George had a lot of friends in San Francisco; he had lived there as hippy in the sixties. Their house was on Potrero Hill, right in the centre of San Francisco and George had asked me if I's like to move in there with him to share the running costs. He told me that it would have been a long commute to the University from Dave's house in Mill Valley and it was just a short bus ride from Potrero Hill. That conversation was way back in Indiana, but now we wanted to stay together for more reasons than just practicality. The conversation we were having here in Utah was quite different as George was talking very seriously about us getting married! He seemed very sincere and was a darling man but I was murmuring gently about my home and family and how difficult it would be to get my student visa extended to enable me to stay in the States beyond December. I remembered that orientation at the YMCA in New York and how it was impressed upon all of us students at the meeting that we shouldn't even think about staying on beyond our visa expiry date and my heart sank a bit!

George reminded me that it was been divine providence that we met and seemed certain that it would all be alright in the end. I just couldn't see how I could make it happen, but I just smiled back at him anyway. I was having a ball, living in the moment, why spoil it with practicalities!

The Dinosaur National Monument on the Colorado/Utah borders was ruggedly glorious with its quarries, canyons and lakes and I was wishing we had more time to explore but we had to keep moving, we had to get to California, we had plans!

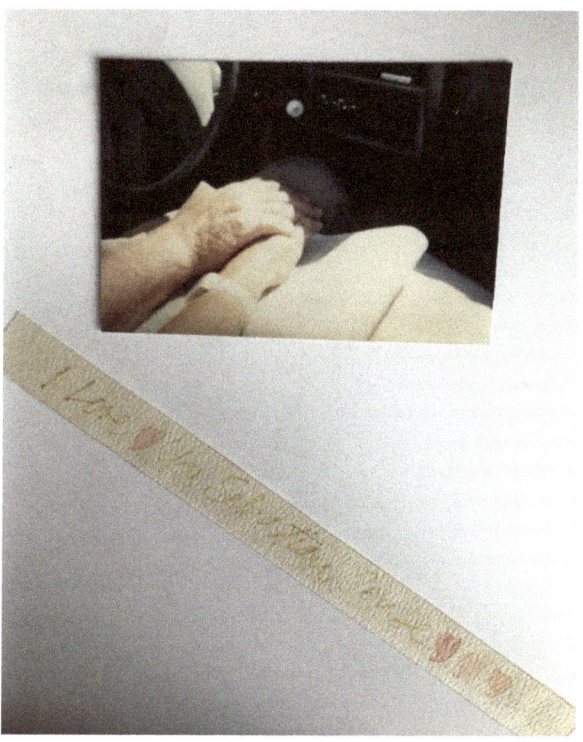

We did however stop for a picnic on the side of the road in a place called, not surprisingly, Dinosaur and it's the place I will always remember George, my giant, proposing to me. He said 'Sebastian, I really do love you and want us to get married.' Sitting at a wooden table in a rest area at the side of the road, in 90F degrees of sunshine in the middle of a desert where some dinosaur bones were found. It was the most romantic thing that had ever happened to me, and indeed, would ever happen. In that moment the only thing I wanted to do was just say yes. So, I said: 'I want us to get married too' and we both sat there grinning like fools. There was nothing else that needed to be said in that moment, just an acknowledgement that we had fallen in love.

We seemed to be driving through cowboy territory now. Red stony deserts and spectacularly huge outcrops of russet rock and no trees at all anymore, with only tumbleweeds rolling across the road. George was driving and instead of looking at the view passing the windows of the dream machine I was just gazing at the profile of this man who had just proposed to me. We'd both fallen silent, lost in our own thoughts following our lovely conversation in that rest area a few miles back. I suddenly had the urge to touch him, so I gently started stroking his big bare arm as he guided the steering wheel. He looked at me and smiled. Then he pulled over, stopped the car and kissed me very tenderly. There were no words spoken. Flippin eck!

We had a bit of time to make up, the glory of the Rockies had caused us to slow down a bit and I had to get to fresher's week in seven days' time! We drove for hundreds of miles through this terrain, making a few comfort stops where there were slot machines in the restrooms. We were clearly in casino country as we headed for Nevada but first, we had to make our way through the Great Salt Lake Desert.

We had been driving all day and were surprised to drive past a couple of camp sites with 'Full' signs outside and as it was starting to get dark, we decided to try and get a room in a place called Wendover, Salt Lake City. We went to a couple of motels and were told we wouldn't get a room for the night because the Bonneville Races were happening. It was an annual event apparently, where racing cars chased each other across the salt flats of Utah.

 The town was heaving, it was clear there wasn't going to be anywhere to stay here tonight. In one last attempt we pulled the Dream Machine into a posh looking hotel, just on the off chance. They obviously weren't used to having a 13-year-old very battered Dodge station wagon pull up outside their hotel with an incongruous couple in it, a little Englishwoman and a great big American man, both a bit scruffy and neither of them dressed for dinner, really! They quickly advised us that they had no vacancies, so we wearily got back into the car, resolving to drive to the next town. But the Dream Machine's battery had died, right there! There was no shifting it from outside of the main entrance of this smart hotel! The horrified concierge quickly found a security guard who had some jump leads and managed to start our car and he then helpfully pointed us towards a garage that would be open. We were very lucky that this breakdown had happened in a town which was totally geared up for cars and racing at this time of the year. The garages were open all night! We went to get something to eat whilst the garage fitted our new battery and checked the car over. The mechanic was incredulous at our answer when he asked, "where have you guys come from". I think he showed our trusty old Dodge a bit more respect once he'd realised how far it had come!

It was becoming clear that we weren't going to find a bed for the night around here, so we agreed to just keep driving across the Great Salt Lake Desert, which was vast and empty. Nothing at all, no lights, no houses, no petrol stations. Just a huge black sky gently lit with millions of stars which seemed to be so close. No light pollution, I felt as if I was under a beautiful blanket. I was sorry it was so dark; it would have been nice to see what I was driving through but it was still a beautiful drive under that star studded night sky. We were struggling to stay awake and George was dozing in the passenger seat. So, that meant that I saw it first. I slammed on the brakes as a huge mountain lion was crossing the road in front of us! He turned his big and beautiful face towards us and stopped for a while, glaring at us as we stared right back, this haughty and handsome beast, his eyes reflecting our lights and then he just walked from one side to the other with his tail outstretched behind him and I swear the length of him from his nose to the tip of his tail took up the whole width of the road. He wasn't in a hurry although he was crossing the road, it was his road after all. We waited for him to disappear into the darkness on the other side of the road before we carried on. One of the many memorable moments of this trip.

We carried on across the desert, without seeing anything else, nothing in the dark for what seemed like hours until we came to the next town to find that they also had no vacancies. We ended up finding a particularly basic camp site and when we got out of the car we found that it was freezing cold. We pitched our tarpaulin to the side of the car and clambered under it. There was nothing for it, to keep warm we shared one sleeping bag, fully dressed and with a lot of giggles as we tried to zip it up! We enjoyed the closeness of our bodies but anything more intimate was impossible, so we just made do with a wonderful horny cuddle. It's amazing what you can get up to when you're still fully dressed and zipped into a sleeping bag with a giant! It had been the small hours of the morning when we found this place and we ended up getting very little sleep as it seemed to start getting light as soon as we dozed off.

>Dinner: $13
Battery: $68
Gas: $15
Oil: $12
Campsite: $8

12. Nevada

We went to a casino for breakfast. It seemed as though everywhere was a casino here on the Utah/Nevada border. Thankfully, I managed a wash in the ladies' room, I was still wearing the clothes I had slept in but at least my face was washed now. I'd never seen slot machines in a ladies' loo before! I did fantasise about putting a few dollars in and winning the jackpot, but money was so tight that I didn't dare risk it.

We were both knackered, we had driven over 400 miles the day before and had got very little sleep last night, what with one thing and another, so we took turns driving and dozing. We took a detour for me in the afternoon, we were quite close to Reno and I wanted to see it. So, we drove to Reno and my first impressions were how tacky it was, with thousands of sequins on the many advertising billboards flashing in the sunshine everywhere I looked. We drove round trying to park, but I had seen enough and so, disappointed with Reno, we hit the road again.

We were approaching California! Sebastian Blue said the elephants were getting excited, just like me. I reflected on our journey, which was almost at an end. It had been a quite an amazing adventure, with many ups and downs, not just the roads we travelled and the places we stayed but with the elderly, oil guzzling Dream Machine. The one constant over the last 3200 miles was my friendship with George, which had blossomed into something more. He had been a wonderful travelling companion, warm, funny, whimsical, affable and gentle. Little did I know when I found him in the forest in Milanville Pa that we would be planning to stay together forever at the end of our journey.

I decided to send Bill Barclay a postcard. I couldn't have done this trip without him! I chose one with a lovely view of the Pacific Ocean on it. I wrote: 'Dear Bill, 3000 miles on the road and I still haven't found a Marks and Spencer! Love Ginny.' I very much doubt if he'd had a client like me before.

Breakfast: $6

Gas: $16

Lunch: $10

Gas: $10

13. California

We hit California around teatime after another 240 miles on the road. As expected, it was stunningly beautiful everywhere you looked. We found a pretty little motel with a pool in a place called Nevada City. We had a lovely swim, then a shower and a welcome change of clothes and then we took a stroll through this pretty little town. We found a restaurant with a garden area where we had a super dinner whilst the sun was setting and George filled me in about the people I would be meeting tomorrow.

He had a couple of old friends who lived in Mendocino, on the Pacific coast to the north of San Francisco. He told me that he had been in a hippy commune with them in the sixties and was really looking forward to seeing them again. One of their sons was getting married in a couple of days at their house, intriguingly called Schooner Gulch House and George had been invited to the wedding. So, that would be where we were heading the next day. It was about a 200-mile drive from where we were now, just a short hop for us by now!

We left Nevada City after breakfast, feeling refreshed after a great night's sleep and we began our drive through California with its rolling hills, winding roads, giant redwood trees and of course, blue, blue skies and sunshine. The countryside looked parched, and it was extremely hot. When we stopped for lunch, our waiter kept making jokey remarks about George's size and George seemed to snap eventually and got very annoyed. I'd never seen him like that before, it hadn't occurred to me that my gentle giant was capable of losing his temper.

Breakfast: $6

Motel: $38

Lunch: $10

Dinner: $35

Gas: $15

I had my first ever view of the Pacific Ocean after lunch. George was amused when I insisted that we stop for a minute so that I could take it in and then I got emotional. It was magnificent, I was overwhelmed that I was actually here.

At the ocean we turned right to Mendocino. San Francisco was just down there to the left, but it would have to wait a couple of days.

We reached Schooner Gulch House at about 5pm. It was a fabulous, sprawling wooden building with a veranda most of the way around it in a massive area of land with a herd of wild deer wandering through it and with stunning views of the Pacific Ocean. George was welcomed with open arms by many of his old friends who were gathering there for the wedding. They were all lovely people, but I found it a bit of strain, I was hot and sticky and tired and felt a bit of a mess. I was not at my best for being introduced by George to a crowd of his old friends as his fiancée and straight away it felt like I was under scrutiny.

Peter and Lesley, the lovely couple who owned Schooner Gulch House had given us a trailer in the grounds for the duration of our stay. George went off with the 'boys' for a bachelor party so I turned in early. It was odd being without him for the evening.

The next morning I was driven to the local launderette by Katryn, another wedding guest, who was clearly very fond of George. I was pleased to spend some time with her because I felt her curiosity and suspicions about me. While we were waiting for our clean clothes, she talked of George with great affection, and I filled her in a bit about me and I think she felt more reassured after our girly chat.

Katryn and I got back to Schooner Gulch house in time for a wedding rehearsal which lasted for most of the afternoon. It felt very strange not having George around me for most of the day. He was with a bunch of old friends and was flitting between them like a butterfly all day. I kept busy with my camera, all the while trying to blend in with this crowd of lovely strangers.

That evening was better though with a wonderful home cooked meal around a huge table and lots of Californian wine flowing and I felt more accepted. Then the joints were passed around and everybody loved everybody else, and I learned that George is very funny when he's stoned! But then, I was laughing at pretty much everything anyway! This was certainly Californian!

The next day dawned, predictably hot and sunny and we were up early for breakfast at the house, which was a hive of activity as we helped to get the garden ready for the wedding which was to happen later on that day. When it was clear that we couldn't do anything else to help, we decided to get out of the way, and we went off for a drive around Mendocino which is rich with giant redwood forests, mineral springs, vineyards and national parks along the Pacific coastline and it became clear that a day wasn't going to be nearly enough time in this wonderful place Also I felt strangely comforted by just being back in the Dream Machine with my giant, just the three of us.

George was getting hungry again, so we stopped for a burger overlooking the beach and then we headed back to the house to get ready for the wedding which was to be later that afternoon on the porch. The wooden porch had been covered with hundreds of wildflowers, sunflowers, grasses, cornflowers and poppies. The bride had about ten bridesmaids in pretty floaty dresses with wildflowers in their hair and the groom had his three brothers and a couple of other guys attending him, all looking great in their suits and psychedelic ties. They were all very handsome and bronze with stunning white even teeth and they looked like an interchangeable set somehow. The whole garden was full of people and the wedding was a very emotional affair with the bride and groom reading each other poems that had everybody in tears, including George and I and as the sun went down on this setting, I decided this was the most beautiful wedding I had ever been to.

Then it was party time and music was playing, the wine was flowing and there was a bit of a haze over the proceedings as spliffs were lit and shared around the crowd. There were trays of delicious food being passed round and tall candles were lit as the sun finally descended over the Pacific Ocean. Everybody was very relaxed and happy and at one point I found myself dancing with George's friend Peter, George didn't like it at all and took me off into a quiet part of the garden and we had quite an argument about it, I didn't understand what the problem was, but George was adamant I shouldn't have danced with Peter like that. I got quite upset about this sudden change of atmosphere between us, but we talked it through and put it down to cultural differences. It was a confusing and disappointing ending to what had been a perfect day.

14. San Francisco

This was the day we would arrive in San Francisco! The end of our journey! I had mixed feelings about that, the trip had been memorable, scary at times, but mostly beautiful, romantic and great fun and I was sad that it was ending, although it would be good to be settling in one place for a little while. The added bonus to that was that I would still be with my big man, I felt very safe with him and he was so happy I would be helping him housesit. I was looking forward to getting to SF State University too, all of a sudden, after months of planning that had started long before I left the UK, that was tomorrow!

George and I met up with a bunch of people from the previous day's wedding party for breakfast at a wonderful restaurant overlooking the Pacific Ocean. George, as usual, ate enough breakfast to last him all day!

As we said our goodbyes to this lovely bunch of Californians, I was pleased it would be just me and my giant again, driving the very last leg of our journey in the Dream Machine, 150 miles or so. Just a short hop for us!

A very pretty run along the coast, I was grateful to George for driving so I could just take in the view, and of course take a few pictures. We hit the freeway into the city and made a stop so that I could take over the driving for that final stretch, over the Golden Gate Bridge. I had to do that! I got quite emotional as I was driving over it, wishing my kids were in the back seat of the Dream Machine to share this fantastic experience with me. I'd only ever been travelled abroad to Spain a couple of times before in my previous life and just look at me now, driving across this iconic bridge into one of the most fabulous cities in the world! No wonder I had a lump in my throat. Was this really me?

When we'd crossed the bridge, I let George get back behind the wheel so that he could negotiate the busy roads and find the house. 953 Kansas Street, Potrero Hill was a pretty little house with an art studio attached, which George was very excited about. It was on the top of a hill and offered marvellous views across the city right to the Bay. I felt very fortunate when I saw the house, it looked sweet, and I felt I would be happy here whilst I was studying.

Breakfast: $12

Gas: £15

Lunch: $13

When we arrived, George's friends, Joseph and Michael, also artists, who were due to fly to Greece in a couple of days, weren't at home. That was ok though; we took a nice stroll around the neighbourhood to stretch our legs and they soon turned up and welcomed us into their home. Once again, I was introduced by George as his fiancée, which seemed to surprise them, but then I was still finding it a bit surprising myself.

All the walls of this sweet little house were lined with massive disturbing portraits of ugly women with cruel cold eyes. It was odd how every single one had a hardness and a coldness about them that made me wonder if the artist
(Joseph) had a big problem with women, which was reinforced by his icy politeness towards me. They had a cute little white dog which had apparently just been to the groomers before being taken to the airport, she was going with them to Greece. As they introduced her to us, they mentioned that she had been having trouble with fleas all summer but had been treated and was clear now.

The couple cooked us pasta and we had dinner together and they gave us a few notes on the running of the house. We turned in early and I was apprehensive about turning up at University tomorrow and finding my way around and we were all tired, so an early night made sense.

I woke early, as I tumbled out of bed and put my feet on the floor, I noticed with horror about five or six fleas land on each bare foot. That little dog didn't seem so cute now and I made a mental note that we would have to fumigate the whole house once Joseph and Michael were on that plane to Greece tomorrow. I had noticed the night before when I wandered around their small but charming garden and noticed that there was a little stagnant pond with clouds of mosquitoes hovering above it. I wondered if they had followed me from Milanville or whether they were Californian mosquitoes. Wherever they came from, they would probably find me. I would definitely have to find a pharmacy today, for fumigators, insect repellant and bite cream. When I was at the pharmacy I would have to ask about giant sized condoms, this had been a bit of an issue on the trip. When our relationship had progressed beyond friendly cuddles and George decided he wasn't going to be gay anymore, the first thing I'd noticed was that my giant was perfectly in proportion. Very nice thank you, but unfortunately when you're in the desert, on the prairie or up a mountain, extra-large condoms are very hard to come by! Dangerous to risk going without, there was an AIDS epidemic going on and I wasn't that stupid, however hot under the collar I was getting. We'd done everything else you can think of except full blown sex in those motel rooms. I later discovered from a friendly pharmacist that condoms for giants are called 'Magnum'. Just in case you ever need to know.

I was imagining the conversation back home again; if only the kids had known what I was up to!

"So, let me get this right, Mum's sleeping with a bisexual in California in the middle of an AIDS epidemic and is seeing imaginary elephants? We need to get her home straight away and have her sectioned!"

After an early breakfast, George drove me to the University for my first time, armed with a mass of paperwork from Nottingham Trent. Having arrived in this city less than 24 hours before, I didn't have the slightest clue how to get anywhere on a bus at that point, I wasn't sure where San Francisco State was and indeed where I was, in more ways than one. I was very apprehensive about today and I was sorry to see the Dream Machine's taillights as it re-entered the traffic after dropping me off. George was full of his plans to start looking for work so we both had a big day ahead of us.

Magnums 3 Packs: $30

Flea bombs (3): £40

Jungle formula (large) $10

15. San Francisco State University

Since I'd arrived in the States in June 1990, it seemed to me that everything had conspired in a way to ensure that I'd have a brilliant time. Roger had given me a place to stay and a job in New York. John had invited me to his fabulous home in Pennsylvania where I'd met George. George coincidentally wanted to travel overland to San Francisco at the same time as me. That journey had been beyond a dream come true. And all this was unplanned happenstance and completely wonderful. I had no reason to believe the conspiracy would end now that I was at my destination.

The Student Exchange Department at Nottingham Trent University had just started an exchange programme with San Francisco State and had in fact asked me to be their first student to go there; me being a mature student and better able to cope with any possible teething problems than younger students. But I wasn't prepared for the impersonal, officious, confusing and downright unwelcoming attitude of the international office. Turned out I wasn't enrolled for any of the classes I had booked on, they didn't recognise any of the paperwork I had with me and I couldn't find anyone who gave a damn! Someone clearly hadn't had a memo about welcoming their first ever student from Nottingham Trent University with open arms!

I wandered about the massive campus for a while, getting lost frequently and trying to keep calm until I found the Creative Arts department. Surely there would be someone there who could help me because I wasn't giving up, although it had already been suggested that I go home!

Thank God for a guy call Kip Bacon, who ran the Brown Bag Theatre Company which gave performances every lunchtime to which the audience would bring their lunch, in a brown bag! See? It doubled up as an Advanced Acting Masterclass, so straight away I really wanted a place! I had grabbed a passing student and asked him who was in charge, quickly learning that my English accent is an asset here. He was the first friendly face I had seen since I arrived on this campus. He led me to Kip's office, confiding in me that Kip is an Anglophile and has Welsh ancestry. At last, a point in my favour in this unexpectedly hostile place! After a little wait outside of his office, I was invited in. I told him about my background and the problems I was having getting enrolled as an exchange student and he didn't seem surprise, which was interesting. I somehow slipped into the interview that my grandad had been a referee at Cardiff Arms Park! That swung it! He accepted me into the Brown Bag! He asked me to attend an audition in a couple of days, with my own audition piece, but first I had to get myself officially registered as a student and he wished me luck with that. I was very grateful and said I would, somehow. And I made a mental note to prepare an audition piece, not having a clue what to do!

I had spent most of the day finding my way around the massive campus and not getting accepted anywhere. I felt very confused, stressed and upset with this whole rigmarole, and very, very lonely. I didn't even know the right bus to catch to get me back to Potrero Hill! It was exhausting.

I hopped on a bus, hoping it was the right one and as it meandered through the streets of San Francisco I did some thinking about my situation. Today had been such a massive reality check. The holiday was definitely over and what a disappointing end to a wonderful trip it had been. Just for now I wasn't sure what was going to happen next. I had found a payphone on the campus and, armed with about 1000 cents to pay for the call I had managed to put a call in to the student exchange office at Nottingham Trent University. I had to leave a message, I had forgotten about the time difference and the office was closed. I told them I was in trouble and urged them to please call the office here at SF State and remind them that they should be looking after me and helping me to get on to the classes I had signed up for three months ago, when I was still in the UK. I resolved I would have to go back to the office tomorrow, armed with my paperwork again and just not leave until they had registered me. Then I would be able to get into the Brown Bag and the other classes I wanted. Which was why I was here.

I arrived back at Kansas Street completely drained. It was Joseph and Michael's last night, they were heading off to the airport early the next morning, their fleabag had already gone to the pet transporter. George was cooking dinner for us all which turned out to be a convivial affair with many 'bon voyage' toasts, the couple were excited about their trip to overwinter in Greece. Apparently, they've got a place there. I wondered whether that place was infested too? The couple had maintained their icy politeness towards me since we arrived and although I was grateful to them to have their potentially lovely home to stay in, I would be glad when they had gone, so that George and I could give this neglected cottage a good clean and fumigation and be comfortably just us again.

He'd asked me a couple of times if I was ok but there wasn't really the chance to tell him about the horrific day that I'd had with Joseph and Michael there. I just said the day had been very tiring and went to bed early and left him chatting with his old friends. I was asleep before he came to bed.

I was up and out early the next day, just knowing where the bus stop was felt like a massive step forward at this stage!

I spent most of the morning 'standing in line' trying to talk to people about staying on. It was starting to look impossible, there was so much more paperwork they seemed to need from me just to accept me, that I just couldn't give them. Seems my student exchange office back home may have slipped up as well as this office being extremely officious and unhelpful.

It was starting to look as if I may have to go home but I really didn't want to leave George just yet. I was really torn between my emotional attachment to him and being unable able to cope with this chaotic school situation and I wasn't about to give up my studies. I just didn't know what to do or which way to turn.

I fell asleep with sheer exhaustion when I got home. George was there but he was also asleep. When we both surfaced a couple of hours later, I made us some dinner out of what I found in Joseph and Michaels cupboards. We realised we would have to go to a supermarket tomorrow. I was still paying all our bills. I had stopped keeping an account of what I was spending on our joint expenses, there didn't seem much point. I trusted George to get work and take over some of the expenses. I was still waiting for my termly grant to be paid into my new Wells Fargo bank account, I had at least managed to open that at the campus branch on my first day, my only achievement. But as of yet, the account was empty. It also seemed George had decided not to start looking for work yet, after all. He had instead started painting a watercolour in the studio in the garden. He proudly showed it to me. It would be beautiful when finished, but it wasn't going to get us round Walmart tomorrow.

I was too stressed to even talk. George didn't really know what to say to me, he'd never seen me like this before. We finished up the wine left from last night and I started telling him about my problems at SF State and how I might have to go home but that I didn't wanted to leave him and then I started to cry.

A cuddle and a 'there, there' would have gone a long way at this point, but instead George got quite cross with me, saying that I had unburdened all of my stress on him, which then made me feel worse. He shouted, 'I want my old Sebastian back!' my gut reaction was, 'This is real life George,' which was like a slap in the face for both of us. He wanted the happy and carefree Sebastian Cerise that Sebastian Blue had fallen in love with, and so did I, but real life had kicked in and I was full of doubts and fears. I feared both Sebastian's had been left on the road together with the elephants. My predicament was not his fault, but it seemed my big gentle George was not as sympathetic as I'd expected.

16. The Dilemma

The next day was slightly less stressful. I'd had a message from the exchange office in Nottingham to say they're working on my problems and to hang in there. I decided to do just that and gave myself the day off from traipsing round the Uni and standing in line. My giant and I were friends again and we gave the cottage a damn good clean. We carefully took down a lot of the massive paintings of ugly women with cold eyes which covered the walls, which we both found disturbing and stacked them away, out of sight. I'd bought some fumigator bombs which would hopefully get rid of the thousands of flees infesting every room so and once we had cleaned everywhere we activated the bombs and went out and left them working their magic, hopefully. Very satisfactory!

This wonderful, surprising romance I was having had proved a great distraction. The last two days of struggle had sharply reminded me of the importance of continuing my studies. I had given up so much to get on this degree course. I would, of course, need to go home in three months, at Christmas. I was very torn; I really didn't want to leave George behind. We had become so close in such a short time and I believed our relationship was meant to be. As he'd described our meeting back at Innisfree, 'divine providence,' we had touched on him moving to the UK with me but we both knew it wouldn't work for many reasons. Why would anybody want to leave California to live in Nottingham? I could see that it wasn't an option. Apart from my studies in Nottingham, I also had my kids who were practically grown up, but they were still my boys who I had brought up on my own since they were in infant school. John was ok, he was living with his dad in Cambridge and working for him, as he had done since he had left school. Tom was still in Nottingham and a student, like me, and I should have been there offering support, rather than swanning off to America and sending him a postcard saying I wasn't coming home! It just wasn't going to happen.

I decided to shelve all this heart searching for now and go back to living in the moment in this fabulous city, which I hadn't had time to explore yet.

I was determined to have a nice day with George. It was important after all the stress I had brought into this relationship over the past couple of days. He showed me Chinatown and the Haight Ashbury, which is a remarkably quirky place where the hippy era started in the 60s. He was there then and had lived in a commune for a while, practising peace and love. It had been a life of sex and drugs and rock and roll and oh how I wish I'd been there too! What completely different lives we had both lived.

It had been a good day all in all, we got back to our nice clean cottage, unpacked the few groceries I had been able to afford, cooked dinner and rolled about in bed for a while until we both fell asleep, smiling.

Tomorrow is another day.

17. Journeys End

Back at University the next day and I found my paperwork was miraculously in order all of a sudden! Seems the student exchange office back home had sent an assertive fax, phew!

First thing I did was go and find Kip Bacon to tell him I was now registered as a student and could join Brown Bag, which was a great relief. Then I stood in line for what seemed like the rest of the day to get myself enrolled into two more classes and to buy the books I needed.

I joined a class called Art of Comedy, which looked interesting, and I also joined a colour photography class. I still felt very much like a stranger in a strange land here amongst this crowd of students milling about, who were half my age, but told myself it would be better when the classes actually started next week.

George was pleased to see me a bit happier that evening and after we had dinner we went out for hot chocolate and cake.

We drifted into a daily routine over the next couple of weeks of coming together for dinner and then going out for coffee and dessert. It was pleasant enough and we were rubbing along together ok, but it wasn't as romantic anymore. And we were so broke! George had been painting while I was at Uni, but I don't think he'd had any luck finding an outlet for his art and there hadn't been much job hunting going on.

We were starting to drift apart. We had our own things to do separately now. Brown Bag Theatre Company and my other classes were keeping me very busy, and George was painting. We didn't have much time left for frivolity and it was affecting our relationship. The fleas had returned to Kansas Street and I had taken to sleeping in the bed up in the loft, where the fleas didn't reach; George chose not to join me. Goodness knows what had happened to all those Magnums I had bought with great anticipation of using them just a few weeks ago.

Whatever money I had left was dwindling away and George was still depending on me entirely for money. I had stopped noting down my daily expenses, I'd realised there was no point. Just before my grant landed in my bank, I was down to $4! We really needed to sell the Dream Machine now.

We had a lovely long drive down the Pacific Highway to Santa Cruz where we watched pelicans diving for fish and seals playing in the sea. It was almost like old times, but not quite. Then we had to stop for food again. George's total preoccupation with food was becoming tedious, as well as expensive and his stomach was growing in front of my eyes. He had acknowledged that he had a problem and said he was going to join Overeaters Anonymous.

That was to be our last journey in the Dream Machine. We had agreed back in Milanville that we would sell the car when we arrived here and that was George's job for tomorrow. Our wonderful Dream Machine had coughed and spluttered and rocked and rolled all the way across America, guzzling oil every step of the way. Because of the weight of all our worldly goods in it, the poor thing struggled to get over 60mph without swaying from side to side, so of necessity it was a slow journey, which was fine with me. Once, we had driven over a dead skunk and the stink in the car had lingered all the way to the next state. This Dodge had a bench seat that was too small for George and too big for me and it didn't lock all the way round. But it had got us here and we had fallen in love with it and its circling elephants as well as each other on the way. I would be sad to see it go; it would mark the end of an era.

The car was sold a couple of days later and George did miraculously well to make $600, which was what we'd paid for it! It had magically held us close as it had carried us here and now it was gone, and so had the magic.

I was shocked when George didn't want to give me my half of the money back and we had a real argument about it. I'd given him $300 way back in Milanville. I had been keeping him and the Dream Machine going since he ran out of money in Nebraska. If I'd had the money, I would have gladly funded the whole trip, I was having a ball in what had been great company. But the whole point of us travelling together was to share the expenses, as we'd discussed and agreed on when we first started talking about travelling together.

I'd had a few warning bells when we looked around for an apartment to live in when the housesitting stint had ended. The smallest one we'd seen was $600 a month plus a $600 deposit. I'd asked how we were going to pay the rent and he said, 'I figured we'd just use your money until it ran out and then think of something else'. Hmm. I had barely enough money to keep myself going, with the addition of funding a gas and oil guzzling old jalopy of a car as well as feeding a compulsive overeater. I thought George had understood that.

Things were never the same after that row, sadly. I was very busy with rehearsals, which often ran into the night, and learning lines which kept me busy when I was at home. Brown Bag loved my English accent and I kept getting parts, which was I was loving, but it was very demanding and didn't leave much time for anything else except for the other classes I was enrolled in. George was often out somewhere when I got home and didn't come home until late. I went out the next morning before he got up and that set the pattern for a couple of weeks. I was also looking for some kind of work that I could fit in with my rehearsals and photography projects.

Then one evening George came home from wherever he had been and asked me to sit at the table with him. He announced that he was now gay again, we were no longer in a relationship and if I wanted to carry on living with him, I would have to pay him rent. In this cottage that he was housesitting for friends, rent free. I reminded him that I had been supporting us since Nebraska and he replied he wouldn't have come to San Francisco if it weren't for me so it was only fair that I should pay for everything! He had apparently forgotten the promise he'd made me back in Nebraska to pay me back his half of our expenses when he insisted on me keeping an account in my diary!

I was taken back to that first weekend at Innisfree when I met him. We were round the dinner table with Bud and Ann Rue and their son John and I was talking about my fall semester at San Francisco State University and how I would like to get here overland. I remember George jumped in, he had been invited to a wedding in Mendocino and also had some friends who needed a house sitter in San Francisco, and he was wondering how to get there and why didn't we buy a car together and drive and share the expenses of the journey. Maybe we wouldn't have made this journey if it hadn't been for that conversation, but there is no doubt that he had his reasons for making it. Surely, he hadn't just been doing me a favour! Or was he just after me for the money he thought I had? His arguments justifying his behaviour were so unreasonable that there was nothing I could answer with. I just asked if it was ok if I could stay until the end of the month and scrambled up into the loft and cried myself to sleep. I was devastated. How disappointing that our wonderfully romantic trip had ended with a car crash like this.

My own little house, my kids and all those lovely friends who'd waved me off from Nottingham what seemed like a lifetime ago, were 6,500 miles away. The only person I knew in this foreign city had inexplicably turned hostile.

The next morning, I woke up to find a note asking me for a month's rent in advance. I left the house before he woke up and arrived at Brown Bag very stressed and tearful. I needed to leave, I didn't know this man anymore, and I didn't know where to go.

Milos, the director of the play I was performing in that lunchtime noticed I wasn't myself and took me outside for a chat. We sat on the steps in the sunshine, and I told him the story. He was horrified! Of course, one sympathetic shoulder and I was sobbing! I said it would be better if I just went home now. After the play, which went surprisingly well in spite of my lack of focus, he introduced me to his sister, Bojana, who lived in Berkeley. He'd told her my story and over lunch she kindly offered me a room until I could find something else. I had an open plane ticket to Heathrow so I could go home any time I wanted. But to leave San Francisco halfway through my course would be an epic failure (especially after the fight I had to get on it in the beginning!) and I would be letting my University down as well as myself. I was so grateful to Bojana and I gladly accepted her offer and Milos offered to drive me and my belongings to his sister's apartment at the weekend.

The few days George and I had left together passed with avoidance and icy politeness. I'd told him I would pay me rent weekly and left him some money, to keep hostility at a minimum. He'd also demanded half of the water bill which had come, so I gave him that too. I felt threatened and uncomfortable around him now. What had happened to this big friendly cuddly man, capable of such tenderness, who I had fallen in love with a few thousand miles ago?

I didn't want him to know I was moving out in case things got nasty, he was suddenly very unpredictable. I arranged with Milos that I'd phone him when George was out on the next Saturday and he would come and get me. I was surreptitiously gathering up my belongings and moving them up to my loft bedroom, where George never came anymore, and packing them away. Saturday morning came and I was putting on a show of my own, acting at learning my lines in the garden. Although my stomach was churning so much that I was surprised George didn't hear it! We had a frostily polite chat and he announced he was going out for the afternoon. As soon as the door closed behind him, I was on the phone to Milos and finishing my packing while I waited for this knight in shining armour to rescue me. And I escaped!

I left a note: "Dear George, I'm sorry it has ended this way, I have been very upset by your recent behaviour, but I hope we'll be friends again one day," or something along those lines.

And that was the end of my wonderful journey with my giant who I had found in the woods. I wondered if he would be happy to find me gone when he got back. This relationship was never going to last, but I was sad that we hadn't parted as friends.

Bojanna, Milos' sister and her husband made me very welcome in Berkeley, and I stayed in their tiny, chaotic and undomesticated apartment for a couple of weeks. There wasn't really room for me and all of my stuff, and it was an hour and a half commute by train (which went right under San Francisco Bay) and bus to Uni and I had been told never to walk back to their place from the station at night because it wasn't safe, so every night I had to get a taxi from the Bart station to take me the two blocks home! I was grateful to these people, but they'd made it clear that I could only stay until I found somewhere else.

During this time, I was rehearsing for another play. Mary was the director of this play, 'Antigone', with cross gender casting, so I was playing King Creon, which was a great part.

Mary and I became good pals. She seemed to be a bit of a wheeler dealer. When I told her that I was looking for work, she offered me a job on a telephone sex line she worked on! She said they would love my accent and apparently you got a bonus if you could make your customer come in 4 minutes. I wasn't sure if I would be any good at it, I was a deed's rather than words sort of girl! Then she told me about a friend of hers who worked for herself, from home and needed an admin assistant. We met, liked each other straight away and I got the job! $12 an hour for a few hours every week, fitting round my rehearsals. Karen and I spent a lot of time chatting and I said I had to get somewhere else to live really soon and, in that moment, the divine providence returned!

Karen had a friend whose daughter was away at College until Christmas and was thinking of renting her room out until then and she asked if I would be interested! I said of course and right then and there Karen got on the phone to Marcia Quartaroli and arranged to take me over there to meet her! She drove me over to California Street, two blocks away from the Golden Gate Bridge where I met Marcia and viewed her lovely, sparkling clean and cosy home. Her daughter's room was a very girly room with a comfy bed and no fleas! We got on very well, Marcia was a very smart woman, about my age, who worked at the San Francisco Hilton Hotel. I moved in there more or less straight away.

I was so pleased that I hadn't given up and gone home!

I phoned George. Now that I was finally settled, I needed to give him an address to forward my mail. Besides, I did kind of miss the romance with Sebastian Blue. He said on the phone that he'd had a bad time because he didn't know where I was, although he admitted he was quite relieved to find me gone when he got home that Saturday. Apparently, there was a lot of mail for me, which he didn't want to forward until I reminded him it was free to forward mail! He mentioned he couldn't pay the phone bill he'd received at Potrero Hill which had quite a few international calls to Nottingham on it. I didn't say anything. I wondered how he was managing for money now that we had parted, but his finances weren't my problem anymore.

Apparently, he hadn't found a job. Instead, he was going to call his old friends in Mendocino to come and get him and take him back to live with them at Schooner Gulch House for a while. This was the kind of man he was, I guess. He had been living with friends in the cottage at Innisfree in Pennsylvania when I first met him, helping out around the place and giving them the odd water colour in lieu of rent. Then he had moved on to housesitting for friends in San Francisco, and now he was planning on staying with his old friends in Schooner Gulch House until it was time to move on to somewhere new. A drifter. Whereas I had roots and responsibilities elsewhere. Our relationship was doomed from the start, really, but it was wonderful while it lasted.

We never saw or spoke to each other again.

I soon settled in with Marcia. We were like minded gals with stories to tell each other and enjoyed going out for breakfast at weekends, taking short walks to the beach right under the Golden Gate Bridge, getting burgers and ice cream delivered and watching old movies together on TCM on Saturday nights together. I was very comfortable comfortable there for the rest of my stay in San Francisco.

Now that I was settled, I was finally able to enjoy the city properly. Uni was still keeping me very busy, but I found the time to camp it up in the Castro, have a good old poke about in the quirky shops in the Haight Ashbury and get the tram to Pier 39, like a tourist, over the next few weeks. I found that just walking about the streets in the winter sunshine was a joyous experience. My birthday in November is usually a gloomy affair, weather wise, but not this year. I'd made a few buddies at University and by now there was always somebody in the campus canteen to share a table with. I was, of course, still skint, but now I only had myself to feed I was able to control my expenses better.

December 1990 came and against all of the odds I had managed to complete my Fall Semester! I achieved good grades. I was able to throw myself into my work without distractions as soon as I had a comfortable place to stay and would be able to walk into Nottingham Trent University in January 1991 with my head held high.

I'd missed my boys terribly and had a great upsurge of joy to see their grinning faces when they met me at Heathrow just after Christmas. My little house had been recently been vacated by my tenants and was cleaned and empty and waiting for me. As was my black cat, Miss Elsie, who'd been living next door for six months and was sitting waiting for me on my doorstep when I arrived at my door for the first time since last June, with a look on her sweet little face that said, 'where do you think you've been?' and she was in the door with her tail up as soon as I unlocked it. I was pleased to be home and I was looking forward to the next chapter in my life as a student.

My boys had been asking me how my trip was, and I'd told them all about my time as a student at San Francisco State. I'd glossed over the rest!

They didn't know that I'd been on emotional roller coaster. That I'd had the most romantic episode of my whole life with a fascinating, whimsical, quirky, unpredictable man who I had shared a magical journey with in our very short but sweet relationship, and who I would never forget. They would never know that I nearly, but not really, left my heart in San Francisco.

Ginny Hartman

January 2021